PETITS JEUX ET ÉNIGMES IN ENGLISH !

de la 6e à la 5e

Sandra Lebrun

HARRAP'S
Le spécialiste de l'anglais !

21, rue du Montparnasse

75283 Paris Cedex 06

HARRAP® est une marque de LAROUSSE SAS.

www.harrap.com

ISBN 978 2 81 870471 4

Direction de la publication : Carine Girac-Marinier
Direction éditoriale : Claude Nimmo
Direction éditoriale adjointe : Stéphanie Auvergnat, Julie Pelpel-Moulian
Edition : Beata Assaf, Giovanni Picci
Conseil pédagogique : Céline Leclerq
Direction artistique : Uli Meindl
Illustrations : Alain Boyer
Mise en page : Loïc Audrain, Tiphaine Desmoulière, Sophie Rivoire
Informatique éditoriale : Dalila Abdelkader
Fabrication : Rebecca Dubois

Remerciements : Sandy Garel, Antonia Skinner

Sommaire

Sommaire

Nice to Meet You!

Tout le monde parle en même temps ! Écris dans l'encadré la lettre qui correspond à la bonne réponse.

1 : 2 : 3 : 4 :

Be Happy!

Dans chaque phrase, barre les lettres en double des mots colorés pour écrire le verbe “to be” conjugué au présent.

I IASMSI A BABY.

THEY IAMREIM HAPPY.

HE AIESAE MY FRIEND.

IT RAIEASER A GOOD FILM.

YOU IASRIES LATE.

WE IMARMIE TOGETHER.

YOU IAMRIME MARRIED.

SHE AIMSAM SLEEPING.

Hello Everybody!

Tout le monde dit bonjour ! Replace dans l'ordre ces quatre façons de saluer au fil de la journée, en commençant par le matin. Relève les lettres dans l'ordre de tes réponses pour compléter la bulle du dernier personnage.

Numbers Puzzle

Relie les nombres écris en lettres de 1 à 20 pour comprendre cette scène.

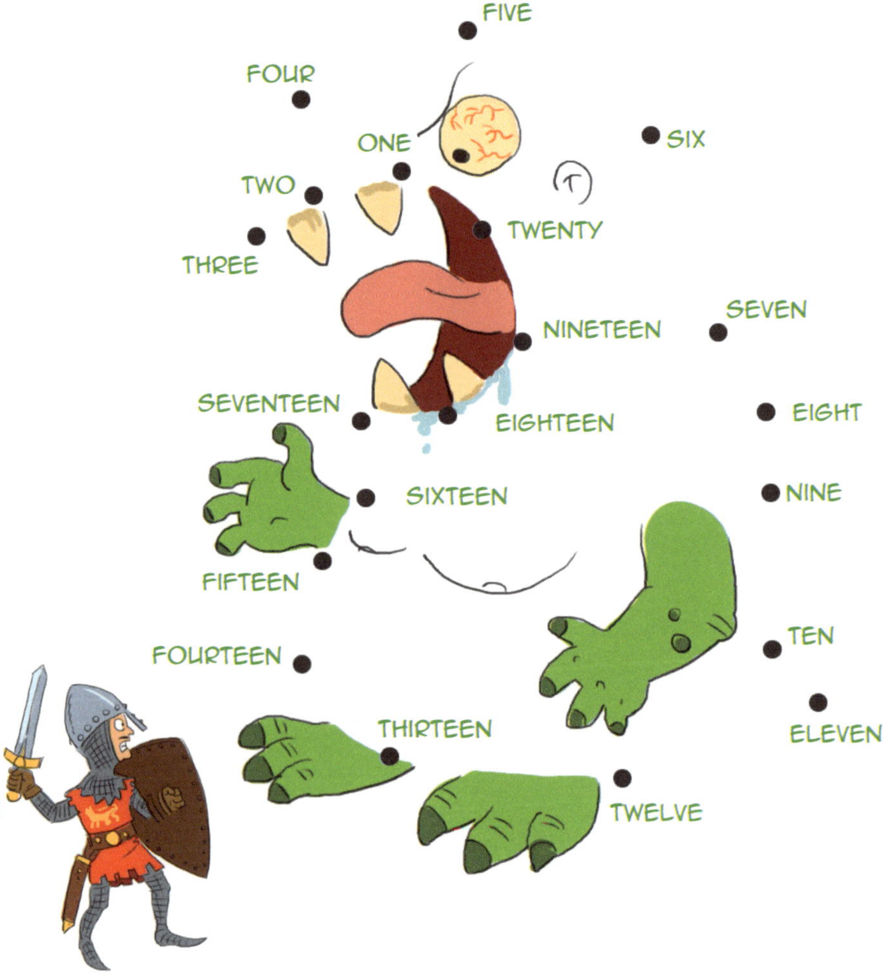

Around the World

Remets dans le bon ordre les lettres des mots écrits en rouge pour découvrir la nationalité de chaque personnage.

Colours

Observe la scène et choisis parmi les couleurs proposées pour répondre aux questions.

WHAT COLOUR IS THE TAXI?

....

WHAT COLOUR IS THE SUN?

....

WHAT COLOUR IS THIS DOG?

....

WHAT COLOUR ARE THESE BIRDS?

....

WHAT COLOUR IS THE SKY?

....

WHAT COLOUR IS THE PHONEBOX AND THE LETTERBOX?

....

WHAT COLOUR IS THE GRASS?

....

WHAT COLOUR IS THE HORSE?

....

BLACK BLUE BROWN GREEN

PINK RED WHITE YELLOW

So British!

Aide-toi du nombre de lettres de chaque capitale pour les écrire sur la carte des îles britanniques.

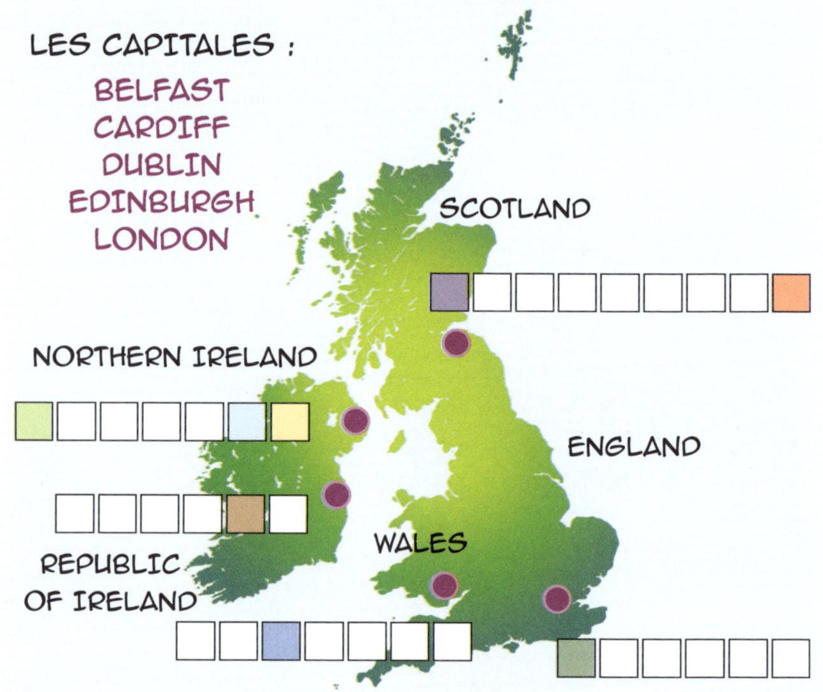

Relève les lettres des cases colorées du jeu ci-dessus pour compléter la dernière addition.

ENGLAND + SCOTLAND + WALES = GREAT BRITAIN

GREAT BRITAIN + NORTHERN IRELAND = THE UNITED KINGDOM

THE UNITED KINGDOM + REPUBLIC OF IRELAND

= _ _ _ _ _ _ _   _ _ _ _ _

Flags

Colorie chaque drapeau en suivant le code couleurs et colorie ensuite le drapeau du Royaume-Uni : "The Union Jack". Que remarques-tu ?

1 = RED 2 = WHITE 3 = BLUE 4 = GREEN 5 = ORANGE

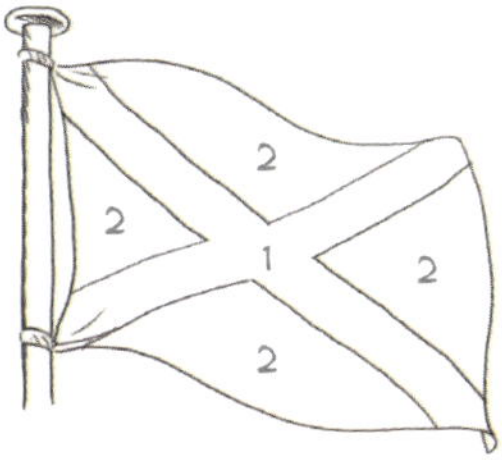

ST. PATRICK'S CROSS
IRELAND

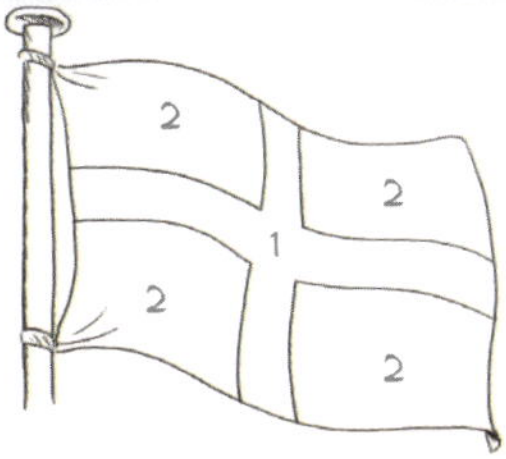

ST. GEORGE'S CROSS
ENGLAND

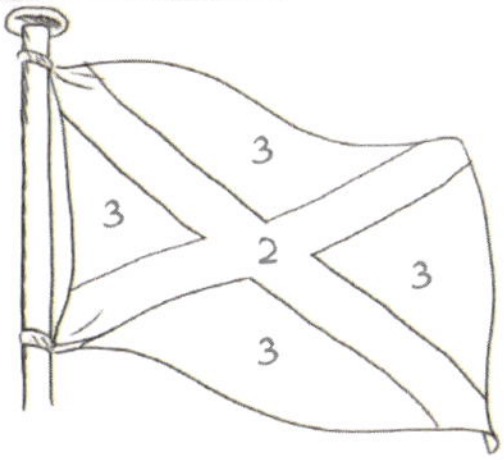

ST. ANDREW'S COSS
SCOTLAND

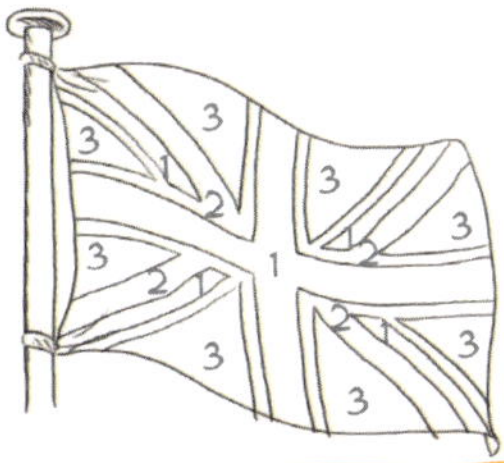

THE UNION JACK
THE UNITED KINGDOM

Garde le même code couleur et colorie le drapeau de la République d'Irlande.

REPUBLIC
OF IRELAND

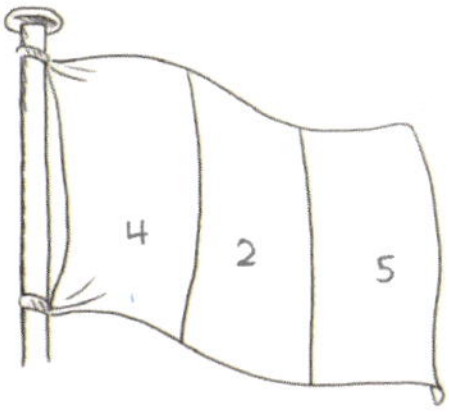

Happy birthday!

Harry attend son anniversaire avec impatience ! Trouve la bonne ombre pour chaque personnage et complète leur bulle avec le mot correspondant écrit en blanc.

Month After Month

Trouve le mois correspondant à chaque définition et écris-les dans la grille. À la fin il te restera un mois. Lequel ?

1 - THIS IS THE FIRST MONTH.
2 - THIS IS THE ELEVENTH MONTH.
3 - THIS IS THE NINTH MONTH.
4 - THIS IS THE SEVENTH MONTH.
5 - THIS IS THE SIXTH MONTH.
6 - THIS IS THE EIGHTH MONTH.
7 - THIS IS THE FIFTH MONTH.
8 - THIS IS THE FOURTH MONTH.
9 - THIS IS THE TENTH MONTH.
10 - THIS IS THE TWELFTH MONTH.
11 - THIS IS THE SECOND MONTH.

THE THIRD MONTH IS: ....

What a Mix-up!

Tous les nombres ordinaux de ces dates ont été notés à l'envers. Écris-les dans le bon sens et relie-les au nombre correspondant.

TUESDAY, THE DRIHT - YTNEWT OF JULY.

T______ ______

MONDAY, THE HTEITRIHT OF SEPTEMBER.

T__________

31ST

23RD

20TH

30TH

SUNDAY, THE TSRIF - YTRIHT OF NOVEMBER.

T______ ______

WEDNESDAY, THE HTEITNEWT OF MAY.

T__________

Four Seasons

Écris dans le cadre la lettre qui correspond à la phrase de chaque personnage qui parle en anglais.

1 : 2 : 3 : 4 :

Photo Memories

Pour chaque photo, choisis la légende qui convient. Relève les prépositions en violet qui correspondent à tes réponses pour compléter les quatre phrases.

EASTER IS _ _ SPRING.

CHRISTMAS IS _ _ DECEMBER, 25TH.

SAINT VALENTINE'S DAY IS _ _ FEBRUARY 14TH.

HALLOWEEN IS _ _ AUTUMN.

Who's Who?

L'inspecteur a pris des notes. Lis ses indices et écris le numéro du suspect en bas du carnet.

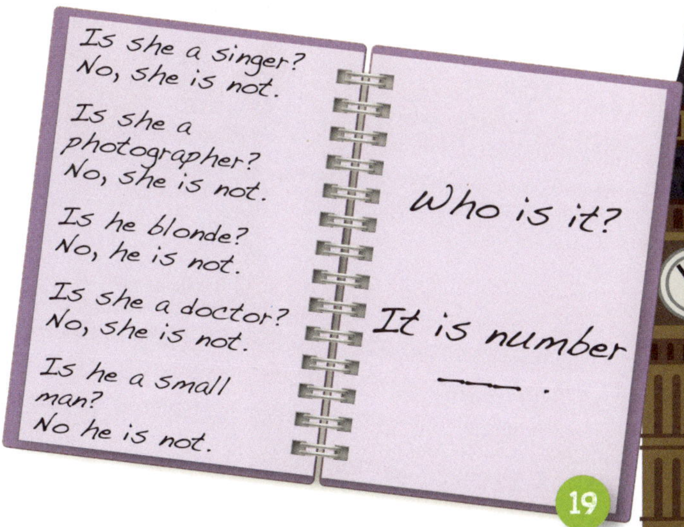

The Royal Family

Aide la princesse Charlotte à compléter son arbre généalogique. Comme sur l'exemple, recule chaque lettre des mots colorés d'une place dans l'ordre alphabétique.

QUEEN ELIZABETH II
PRINCE PHILIP
"OUR HSFBU-HSBOEQBSFOUT"
GREAT-GRANDPARENTS

PRINCE CHARLES
PRINCESS DIANA
"OUR HSBOEGBUIFS"
"OUR HSBOENPUIFS"
_ _ _ _ _ _ _ _ _ _ _
_ _ _ _ _ _ _ _ _ _ _

PRINCE WILLIAM
KATE MIDDLETON
"OUR GBUIFS"
"OUR NPUIFS"
_ _ _ _ _ _
_ _ _ _ _ _

PRINCE HARRY
"OUR VODMF"
_ _ _ _ _

PRINCE GEORGE
"MY CSPUIFS"
_ _ _ _ _ _ _

PRINCESS CHARLOTTE
"I AM GEORGE'S TJTUFS"
_ _ _ _ _ _

Ring! Ring!

Écris dans l'encadré la lettre de la réponse qui correspond à chaque question.

1 : 2 : 3 : 4 :

The Move

Remets les cases de cette BD dans le bon ordre et relève les lettres de tes réponses pour compléter le nom du chien dans la dernière case.

L

- WHERE IS YOUR HOUSE?
- IT IS THIS ONE WITH THE DOG.

O

- NICE TO MEET YOU.
- HOW ARE YOU?
- I'M FINE, THANK YOU.

W

- WHO ARE YOU?
- I'M YOUR NEW NEIGHBOUR.

F

- WHAT IS HIS NAME?
- _ _ _ _ Y!

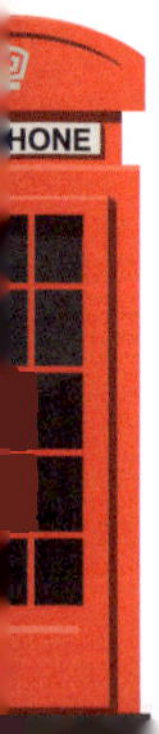

Word Mix

Remets les mots de chaque phrase dans le bon ordre.

GOT A HE BLUE T-SHIRT HAS.

HAT. GOT SHE HASN'T A

THEY A HAVE COMPUTER. GOT

Suis le fil de chaque question pour trouver la réponse qui correspond.

Party!

Barre horizontalement et verticalement chacun des mots colorés dans la grille et relève les 5 lettres restantes pour compléter la bulle du personnage qui lève les bras.

T	H	I	R	S	T	Y
H	H	U	N	G	R	Y
H	C	N	O	I	S	Y
O	A	A	S	A	D	P
T	L	T	I	R	E	D
P	M	Y	C	O	L	D

So Cute!

Harrison a plein d'animaux. Suis chaque chemin et recopie les lettres qui s'y trouvent pour écrire le nom de chaque animal de compagnie.

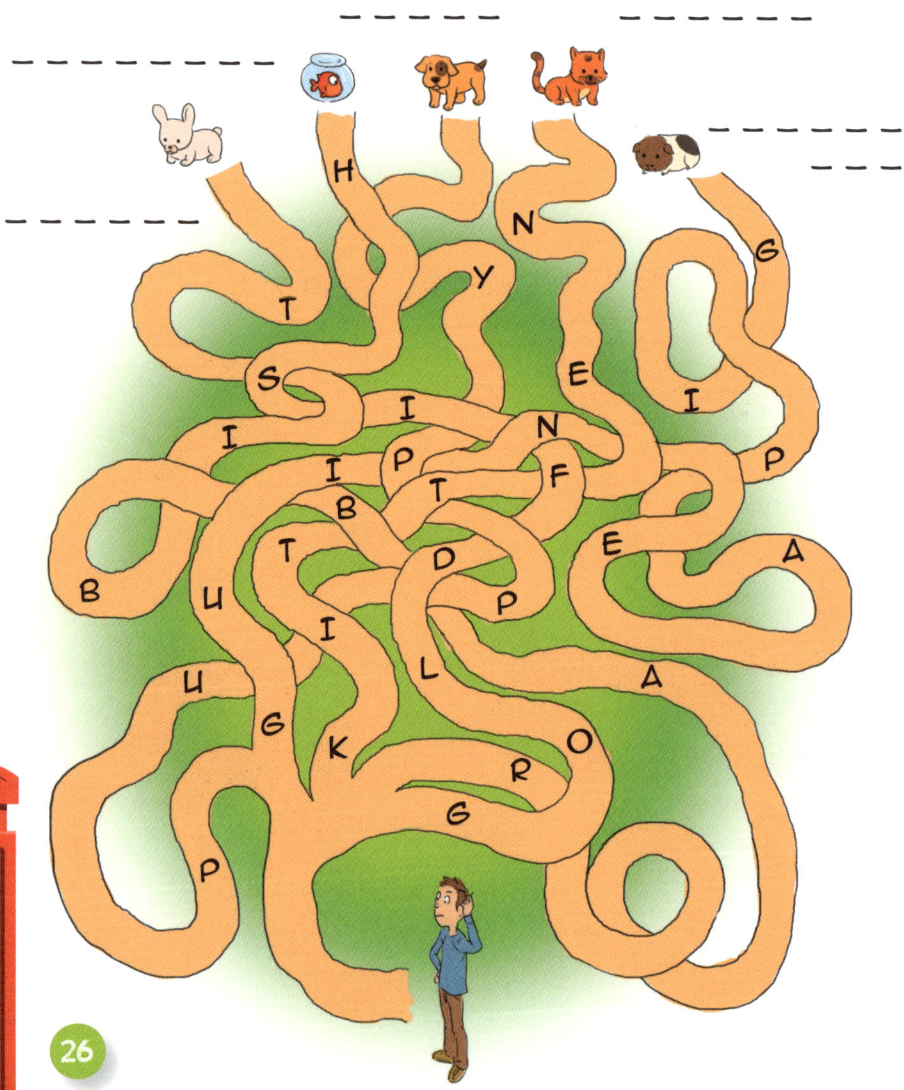

Tweet! Tweet!

Barre les lettres en double dans les mots colorés pour écrire le bon déterminant de chaque phrase.

Jobs

Pour chaque phrase, choisis la case "true" (vrai) ou "false" (faux). Rends au bon personnage la description qui lui correspond.

1

I AM A SECRETARY
AND I HAVE GOT
A COMPUTER.

☐ TRUE ☐ FALSE

2

HE IS A POSTMAN
AND HE HAS GOT
THE LETTERS.

☐ TRUE ☐ FALSE

3

HE IS A CLOWN
AND HE HAS GOT
A RED NOSE.

☐ TRUE ☐ FALSE

4

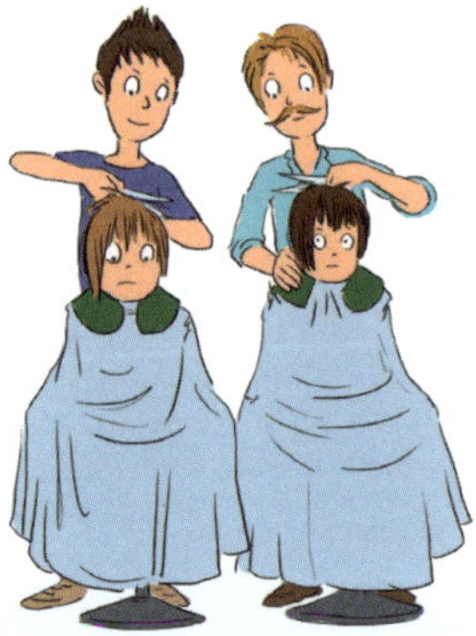

WE ARE HAIRDRESSERS
AND WE HAVE GOT
SCISSORS.

☐ TRUE ☐ FALSE

The Hair Salon

Aide le coiffeur à rejoindre son salon. À chaque fois qu'il rencontre un client, choisis la direction qui permet de compléter sa description.

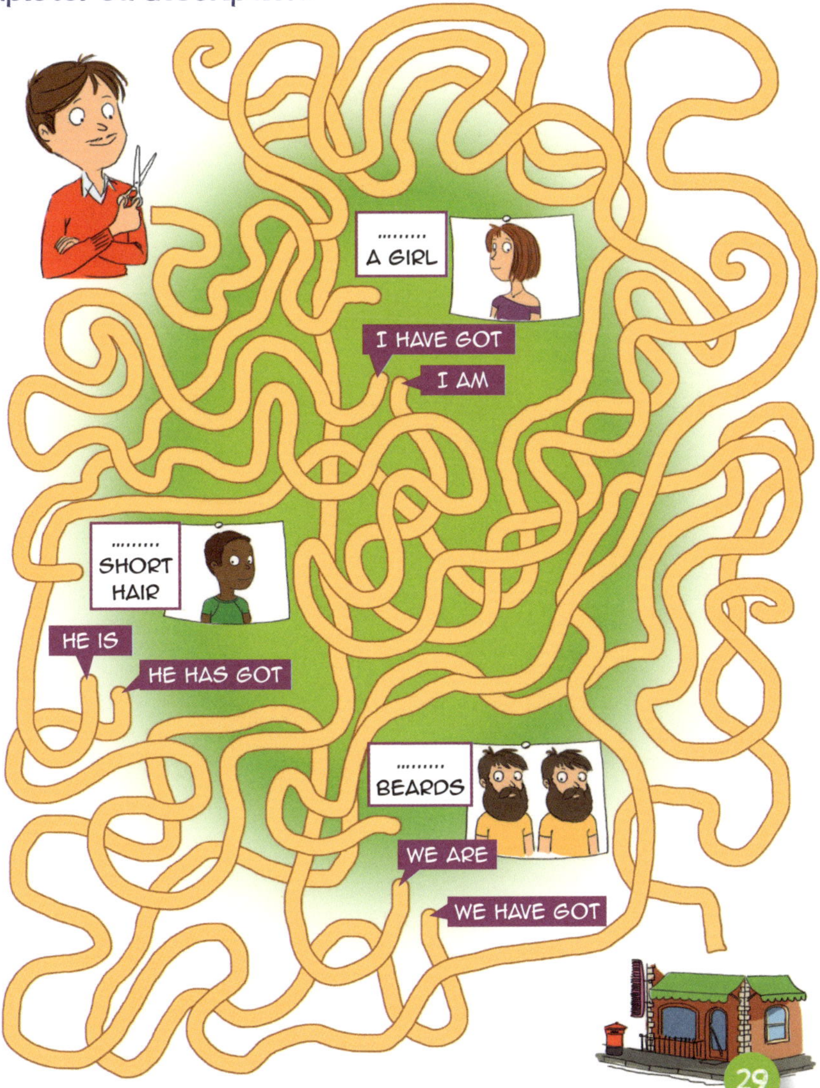

Puzzle

Reconstitue les trois phrases en assemblant les pièces de même couleur. Aide-toi de leur forme pour écrire les mots dans le bon ordre sous l'image correspondante.

1 _ ______ ____.

2 _ __________ ____.

3 _ _____ ___.

My Friends

Remplace chaque nombre par la lettre correspondante dans l'ordre alphabétique pour trouver le déterminant qui convient. Par exemple : 1 = A, 2 = B...

WE ARE GOING
ON FAMILY HOLIDAYS WITH
15.21.18 _ _ _ PARENTS.

THEY ARE RUNNING WITH
20.8.5.9.18 _ _ _ _ _
NEW SHOES.

SHE IS SO PRETTY, I LOVE 8.5.18 _ _ _ EYES.

WHAT IS
25.15.21.18 _ _ _ _
NAME?
MY NAME IS LUKE.

WHO IS WITH JOHN?
IT'S
8.9.19 _ _ _ SISTER.

My Body and my Face

Colorie dans la grille les lettres qui permettent d'écrire les mots fléchés sur le corps de Damien. À la fin il te restera deux cases pour écrire le mot manquant.

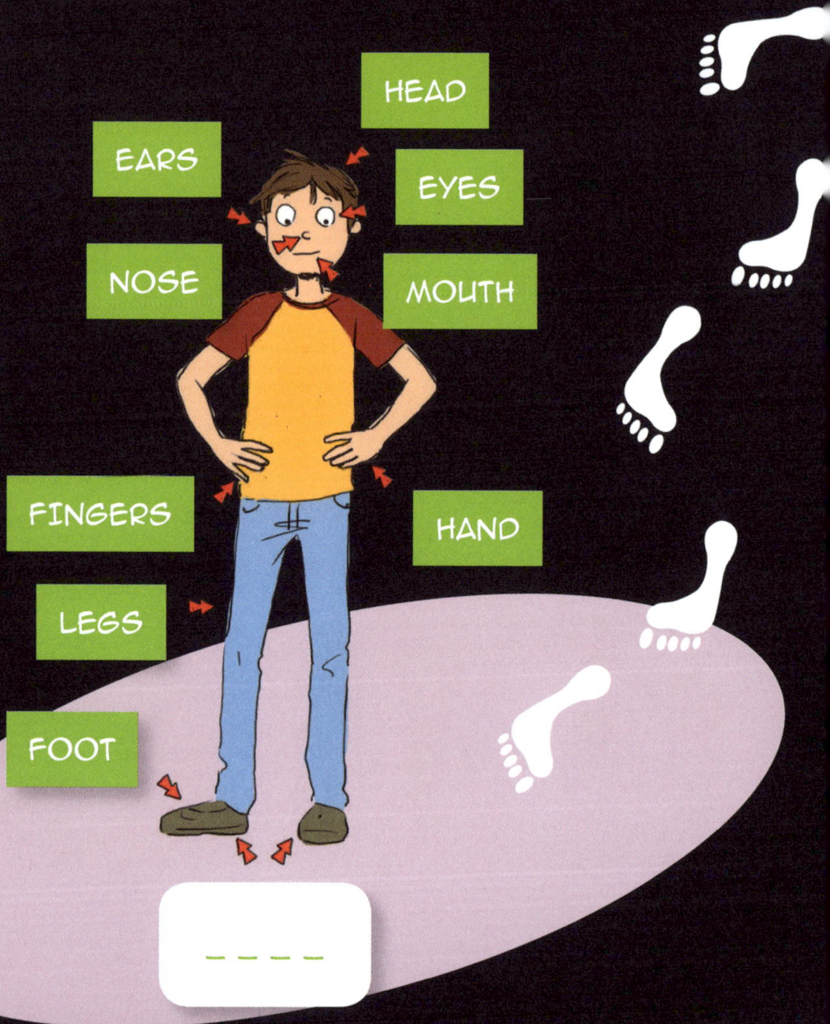

HE	FIN	EA	NO
AD	RS	HA	MOU
FE	SE	LE	ND
EY	FO	GERS	ES
GS	OT	TH	ET

My Look

Rends à chaque personnage la bulle qui lui appartient et écris dans l'encadré le chiffre qui correspond.

A : B : C : D :

Pretty Woman

Joanna ne sait pas comment s'habiller. Aide-toi du nombre de lettres de chaque mot pour les écrire dans la grille et découvre verticalement, dans les cases colorées, le vêtement qu'elle choisira.

Boo!

Entoure l'ombre qui correspond exactement à chaque déguisement pour trouver le nom du personnage.

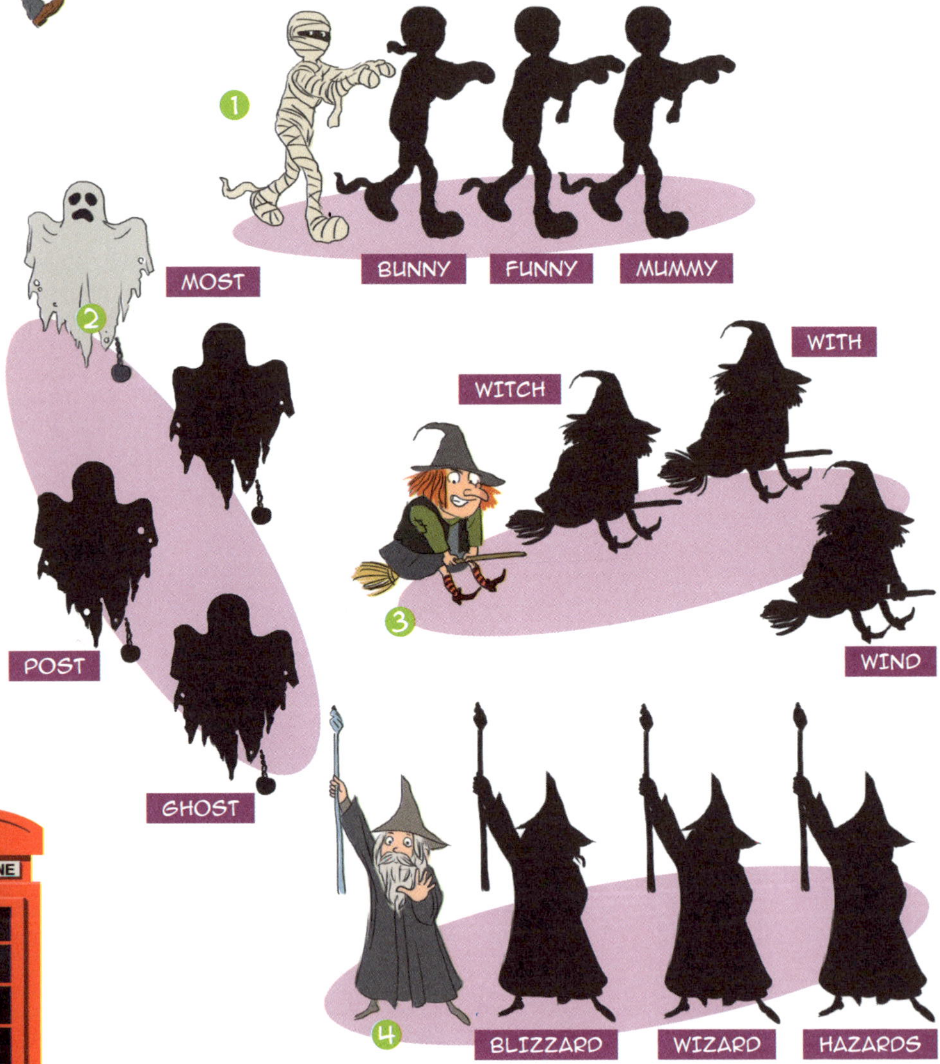

The Match

Trouve la balle ou le ballon qui correspond à chaque sportif pour compléter sa phrase avec le bon mot.

TENNIS GOLF RUGBY FOOTBALL

Music Maestro!

Le musicien cherche son instrument. Trouve le seul instrument qui n'est pas en triple, c'est le sien. Entoure son nom.

FLUTE SAXOPHONE TRUMPET GUITAR DRUMS

HARP VIOLIN PIANO BAGPIPES

English Breakfast

Écris dans l'encadré la lettre de la réponse qui correspond à chaque question.

1 WHAT DO YOU WANT TO EAT FOR BREAKFAST?

2 WHAT DO YOU WANT TO DRINK?

3 DO YOU LIKE ORANGE JUICE?

4 DO YOU WANT SOMETHING ON YOUR TOAST?

A YES I LIKE IT.

B I WANT BACON AND EGGS PLEASE.

C YES I LIKE THIS MARMALADE.

D SOME FRUIT JUICE PLEASE.

1 : 2 : 3 : 4 :

Enjoy!

Observe cette scène et réponds aux questions par vrai ou faux. Relève les lettres de tes réponses pour compléter la phrase de Teddy.

1 – CLARA DOESN'T LIKE CHEESE, SHE SAYS IT'S SMELLY.
C – TRUE M – FALSE

2 – THE FATHER LIKES COFFE, IT SMELLS GOOD.
A – TRUE I – FALSE

3 – THE CAT DOESN'T WANT FISH, IT'S DISGUSTING.
L – TRUE K – FALSE.

4 – TEDDY WANTS SOME MEAT, IT'S YUMMY.
K – TRUE E – FALSE.

Lunchbox

Les ingrédients de ce menu ont été découpés. Remets les bandes dans le bon ordre et note sur le menu les lettres correspondantes.

Free Time

Trouve quelle image correspond à chaque phrase. Puis, écris les lettres sur les tirets verts, dans l'ordre de tes réponses, pour découvrir ce que Théo déteste.

I ENJOY WATCHING TV.

I LIKE READING A BOOK...

...BUT I PREFER SURFING THE INTERNET.

I LOVE LISTENING TO MUSIC.

AND I HATE _ _ _ _ ING.

Pour lire ses préférences, écris les mots manquants en t'aidant du code.

I LIKE  _ _ _ _ _ _ _ _ VIDEO GAMES, IT'S FUN.

I LOVE  _ _ _ _ _ _ _ _ _, IT'S EXCITING.

I PREFER  _ _ _ _ _ TO THE CINEMA, IT'S AMAZING.

I  _ _ _ _ HORROR MOVIES, THEY ARE SCARY.

Balanced Diet

Lis les conseils du médecin et aide Nicole à trouver le repas le mieux équilibré pour rester en bonne santé. Aide-toi des couleurs de chaque aliment.

1

FRUIT JUICE + TOMATOES + ORANGES + PEARS + WATER

2

WATER + SPINACH + FISH + BREAD + YOGHURT + GRAPES

3

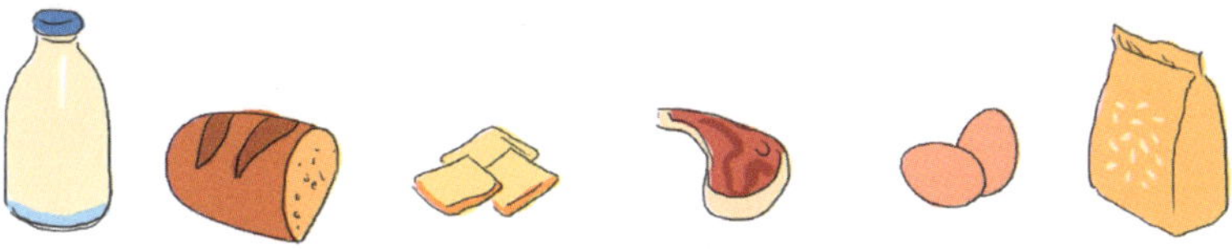

MILK + BREAD + CHEESE + MEAT + EGGS + RICE

Recreation

Pour découvrir la destination de chaque personnage, relève les lettres sur leur chemin et note-les sur les tirets.

_ _ _'_ _ _ _   _ _ _ _   _ _ _ _ _ _   _ _ _ _ _ _ _

Star

Pour chaque phrase, choisis le bon pronom complément et note les lettres des réponses pour compléter la dernière phrase.

1. – DO YOU KNOW THIS MAN?
   – YES I KNOW ....
   T – HIM F – IT

2. – DO YOU KNOW HIS WIFE?
   – NO I DON'T KNOW ....
   U – US R – HER

3. – DO YOU LIKE HIS MOVIES?
   – YES I LIKE ....
   N – ME A – THEM

4. – DO YOU THINK IT IS ME IN THIS PICTURE?
   – NO IT IS NOT ....
   M – YOU N – US

5. – DO YOU THINK IT IS YOU?
   – NO IT IS NOT ....
   Y – HER P – ME

WHO IS HE?
HE IS THE _ _ _ _ _ _ .

Relie les deux moitiés de même couleur de chaque "cracker" pour découvrir ce que Sarah mangera à Noel.

I LIKE _ _ _ _ _ _ _ WITH _ _ _ _ _ _ _ _ _ _ _ _ _ _ _ _ .

AND I LOVE _ , IT'S SO TASTY!

In the Morning

Remets les mots colorés dans l'ordre pour écrire les réponses. Note le numéro correspondant à la pièce de la maison ci-dessous après chaque phrase.

DOES SHE BRUSH HER TEETH IN THE GARAGE?

NO SHE DOESN'T.

THEM BRUSHES SHE IN BATHROOM. THE

.... ☐

DOES HE GET DRESSED IN THE KITCHEN?

NO HE DOESN'T.

HIS HE IN BEDROOM. GETS DRESSED

.... ☐

DO THEY HAVE BREAKFAST IN THE ATTIC?

NO THEY DON'T.

IN THEY BREAKFAST DINING ROOM THE. HAVE

.... ☐

Ready!

Lis les phrases pour remettre les images dans l'ordre. Puis écris les lettres dans l'ordre de tes réponses pour compléter la dernière phrase.

I WAKE UP AT SEVEN O'CLOCK.

I READ IN MY BED FROM SEVEN TO A QUARTER PAST SEVEN.

I GET UP AT A QUARTER PAST SEVEN.

I HAVE BREAKFAST FROM A QUARTER PAST SEVEN TO HALF PAST SEVEN.

I HAVE A SHOWER FROM HALF PAST SEVEN TO A QUARTER TO EIGHT.

I AM READY TO GO TO PLAY FOOTBALL AT EIGHT _ ' _ _ _ _ _.

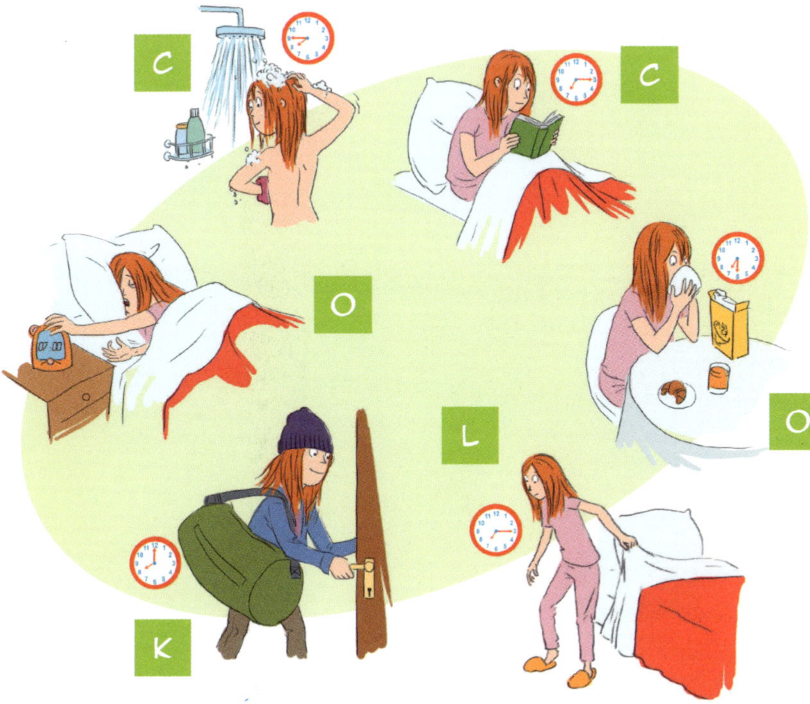

Tick-tock

Relie chaque horloge à l'image qui correspond au même moment de la journée.

04:30 P. M. | 12:00 A. M. | 01:00 A. M.

Sur chaque montre ajoute la grande aiguille.

IT IS TWENTY PAST THREE

IT IS TWENTY TO FIVE

IT IS TWENTY-FIVE PAST ELEVEN

IT IS FIVE TO NINE

When?

Raye une lettre sur deux pour découvrir le mot manquant dans chaque phrase. À toi de trouver la lettre à rayer en premier.

WE
BAILUWTARYMS _ _ _ _ _ _
GO TO BED AT 09:00 P.M.

YOU UNIERVIETRE
_ _ _ _ _
WATCH TV
IN THE MORNING.

HE NOAFLTREUNI
_ _ _ _ _
DOES HIS HOMEWORK
ON SUNDAYS.

SAORMIELTRIUMPETS
_ _ _ _ _ _ _ _ _
WE GO TO THE CINEMA
AT THE WEEKEND.

Housework

Chaque jour, Lisa participe à une tâche ménagère. Entoure les images qui correspondent à ce qu'elle fait chaque semaine. Il restera une image, c'est ce qu'elle ne fait pas.

ON MONDAY,
SHE SETS THE TABLE.

ON TUESDAY,
SHE MAKES HER BED.

ON WEDNESDAY,
SHE TIDIES UP HER BEDROOM.

ON THURSDAY,
SHE CLEARS THE TABLE.

ON FRIDAY,
SHE CLEANS HER DESK.

ON SATURDAY,
SHE CLEANS THE BATHROOM.

ON SUNDAY,
SHE PREPARES A MEAL.

SHE DOES NOT ....

A - CLEAN THE KITCHEN.
B - DO THE WASHING-UP.
C - IRON THE CLOTHES.

Rules

Superpose les deux bulles de chaque personnage pour comprendre ce qu'ils doivent ou ne doivent pas faire.

1

2

3

4

Yes We Can!

Pour chaque scène choisis la bonne proposition. Relève les lettres de tes réponses pour découvrir ce que cherche Léa.

1

HE [T - CAN / W - CAN'T] HEAR.

2

THEY [A - CAN / H - CAN'T] SWIM.

3

HE [T - CAN / E - CAN'T] READ.

4

CAN YOU RUN?

A - YES I CAN

C - NO I CAN'T.

5

CAN YOU PLAY PIANO?

H - OF COURSE I CAN!

N - OF COURSE I CAN'T!

I CAN'T FIND MY _ _ _ _ _

It's not me...

Aide-toi des numéros pour écrire les impératifs dans la grille et lis dans les cases colorées ce que dit le professeur.

Geography

Complète ce sudoku sachant que sur chaque ligne, chaque colonne et chaque carré de 9 cases tu dois écrire ces 9 lettres : AEHKLMOPT.

Relève les cases colorées dans l'ordre, ligne par ligne, pour découvrir ce que dit le professeur.

	A		K		E		H	T
M	P	E	L		H	K		A
	T	H	P		O		M	L
A	O		H	P			K	E
E	M			L	A	H		P
	L	P		K	T	O		M
O	K			E	L		P	H
T	H		A	O		M	E	
		A	M		K	T	L	

Subjects

Quel bazar sur ce bureau ! Un seul livre n'est pas en double, lequel ? Dépêche-toi de le trouver, c'est celui du prochain cours de Malika.

In my Classroom

Observe cette classe et choisis la bonne réponse pour chaque question.

1. HOW MANY PAIRS OF SCISSORS ARE THERE?
   A - THREE   B - FOUR
2. HOW MANY CHILDREN ARE ASKING QUESTIONS?
   A - ONE   B - TWO
3. HOW MANY TEACHERS ARE IN THE CLASSROOM?
   A - ONE   B - THREE
4. HOW MANY PENS ARE THERE?
   A - FIVE   B - SEVEN
5. HOW MANY SCHOOLBAGS ARE THERE?
   A - SIX   B - NINE
6. HOW MANY BOOKS ARE THERE?
   A - NINE   B - ELEVEN
7. HOW MANY RULERS ARE THERE?
   A - FOUR   B - FIVE
8. WHAT COLOUR IS THE DESK?
   A - GREY   B - BROWN

Timetable

Observe l'emploi du temps de Mary et James pour compléter leur phrase avec les bons jours de la semaine.

MONDAY	TUESDAY	WEDNESDAY	THURSDAY	FRIDAY	SATURDAY	SUNDAY
ENGLISH	HISTORY	MATHS	RELIGIOUS EDUCATION	ENGLISH		
MATHS	FRENCH	BIOLOGY	CHEMISTRY	GEOGRAPHY		
LUNCH	LUNCH	LUNCH	LUNCH	LUNCH		
PHYSICAL EDUCATION	MUSIC	INFORMATION COMMUNICATION TECHNOLOGY	ART	PHYSICAL EDUCATION		

IT'S THE WEEKEND

Hide and Seek

Lis les indices et écris le numéro correspondant à côté de chaque animal pour aider Lucas à trouver où ils se cachent.

1. THERE IS A SQUIRREL IN A SMALL TREE.
2. THERE IS A SNAIL ON A STONE.
3. THERE ARE FROGS UNDER A WATER LILY.
4. THERE IS A BUTTERFLY FLYING TO THE LEFT.
5. THERE IS A FOX BEHIND THE BIG TREE.
6. THERE IS A BEAR IN FRONT OF THE BIG TREE.
7. THERE ARE BEES AROUND THE BEAR.
8. THERE IS A BIRD FLYING TO THE RIGHT.
9. THERE IS A RABBIT NEXT TO THE SNAIL.

Food

Écris dans l'encadré la lettre de la réponse qui correspond à chaque question.

1 : 2 : 3 : 4 :

Video Game

Pour comprendre cette scène, remets les mots à l'endroit et complète la réponse avec le bon nombre.

Utilise le tableau de décodage sur l'écran pour comprendre ce que dit Harry.

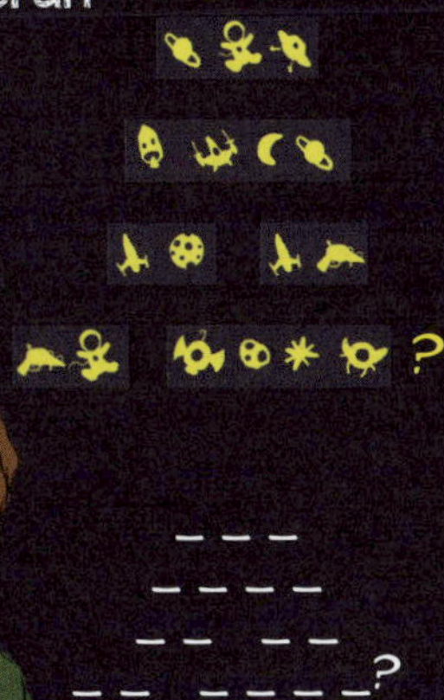

At Home

Note le numéro de chaque personnage dans la pièce où il se trouve, sachant qu'ils ne sont jamais deux dans une même pièce. Complète les phrases avec le bon mot.

1

HE IS IN THE

_ _ _ _ _ _.

2

SHE IS IN THE

_ _ _ _ _.

3

HE IS IN THE

_ _ _ _ _ _ _.

4

HE IS IN THE

_ _ _ _ _.

5

SHE IS IN THE

_ _ _ _ _ _ _ _.

6

HE IS IN THE

_ _ _ _ _ _ _.

7

HE IS IN THE

_ _ _ _ _ _ _.

8

SHE IS IN THE

_ _ _ _ _ _ - _ _ _ _.

9

HE IS IN THE

_ _ _ _ _ _ - _ _ _ _.

ATTIC
BATHROOM
TOILET
STUDY
HALL
STAIRS
BEDROOM
GARAGE
LIVING-ROOM
DINING-ROOM
KITCHEN
GARDEN

In my Bedroom

Écris tous les mots de la liste dans la grille. Relève les lettres des cases colorées pour écrire ce dont Samir aurait besoin dans sa chambre.

Relie les points sur le bureau de 1 à 8 pour découvrir à quoi correspond le mot que tu as trouvé.

In Town

Replace les enseignes au bon endroit dans la ville. Aide-toi du nombre de lettres, des couleurs et de leur ressemblance avec les mots français.

MUSEUM

BANK

CINEMA

PARK

SWIMMING POOL

SUPERMARKET

POST OFFICE

SCHOOL

RESTAURANT

PHARMACY

LIBRARY

A Good Price

Pour aider Anna à poser sa question, relie les lettres en suivant la direction indiquée par la flèche de chaque page. Commence par celle qu'elle tient dans la main.

At the Greengrocer's

Complète les phrases en remplaçant chaque chiffre par la lettre correspondante dans l'ordre alphabétique.

Cheers

Complète chaque phrase avec la bonne proposition et relève les lettres de tes réponses pour compléter la comparaison entre Glen et Nicole.

1

JOHN IS A - OLD / B - OLDER THAN LESLEY.

2

SANDRA IS E - PRETTY / I - PRETTIER THAN DONALD.

3

DIDIER IS MORE G - AMUSING / S - AMUSE THAN LYDIA.

GLEN IS
_ _ _ GER
THAN NICOLE.

Woof and Meow

Gandalf le chien et Maki le chat s'observent. Remplace les chiffres par les lettres correspondantes dans l'ordre alphabétique pour compléter les deux phrases.

THE DOG IS AS
9.14.20.5.12.12.9.7.5.14.20
_ _ _ _ _ _ _ _ _ _ _ _
AS THE CAT.

THE DOG IS NOT
AS 6.1.20 _ _ _
AS THE CAT.

Shopping

Lis ce que dit chaque vendeur et relie-le au magasin dans lequel il travaille pour compléter sa bulle.

I AM THOMAS AND I WORK NEXT TO THE SHOE SHOP. I WORK IN THE _ _ _ _ _ _ _ SHOP.

1

A

I AM JOHN AND I WORK BETWEEN THE SPORTS SHOP AND THE VIDEO GAME SHOP. I WORK IN THE _ _ _ _ _ _ _ _ SHOP.

2

B

I AM ALEX AND I DO NOT WORK NEXT TO THE SPORTS SHOP. I WORK IN THE _ _ _ _ _ _ _ _ _ _ SHOP.

3

C

I AM GEORGE AND I WORK NEXT TO THOMAS'S SHOP. I WORK IN THE _ _ _ _ SHOP.

4

D

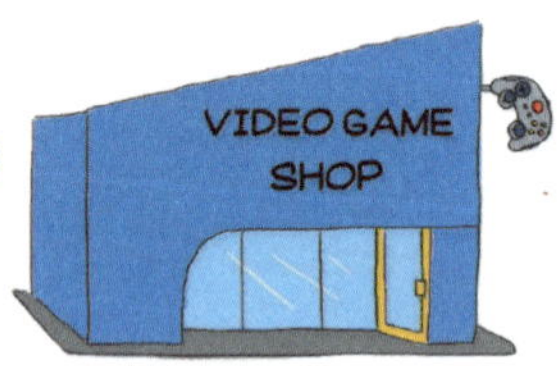

Money! Money!

Sachant que 100 pence (100p) correspond à 1 pound (£1), trouve quelle étiquette correspond au gâteau du même prix puis, relève les lettres dans l'ordre de tes réponses pour savoir ce que Marilou a trouvé.

N £2 Y £10 E £6.50 N £25 P £3

Famous!

Recule chaque lettre d'une place dans l'ordre alphabétique et découvre ce que chantent les Beatles.

Remets les morceaux de la carte postale dans le bon ordre pour découvrir la résidence officielle de la famille royale...

The Weather

Martin n'a pas vérifié la météo avant de partir. Aide-le à aller à Hyde Park et relève les lettres le long du chemin pour découvrir la météo du jour.

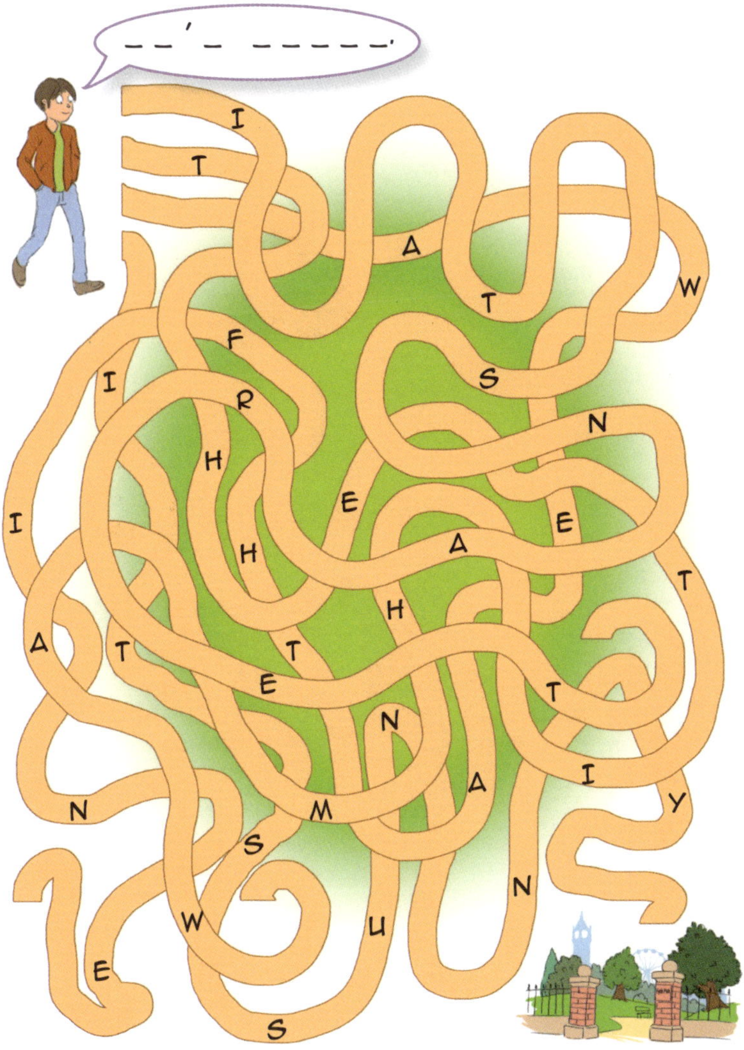

Wow!

Pour comprendre ce que raconte Elizabeth à sa copine, raye une lettre sur deux puis écris la phrase dans l'encadré.

London

Billy a visité Londres. Trouve quelle photo a été prise à chaque moment de sa promenade et écris les lettres sur les tirets violets pour découvrir le lieu où il n'est pas allé. Entoure la photo correspondante.

I

G

A

B

Visit to the Zoo

Observe bien les détails de chaque scène pour numéroter les cases de cette BD dans le bon ordre. Relève les lettres et complète la dernière phrase.

WE TOOK A SELFIE.

WE VISITED THE ZOO.

WE WENT TO THE ZOO ON A RED DOUBLE-DECKER BUS.

WE SAW A GIRAFFE.

WE CAME BACK
IN A BLACK TAXI,
HE _ _ _ _ _ TOO FAST.

Emblems

Relie chaque question à la bonne réponse et complète les phrases avec le prénom et le symbole qui correspond à son pays. Aide-toi des couleurs et du nombre de lettres.

1. WHOSE GREEN SHAMROCK IS IT?
2. WHOSE THISTLE IS IT?
3. WHOSE ROSE IS IT?
4. WHOSE LEEKS AND DAFFODILS ARE THEY?

A. THEY ARE _ _ _ _ _'S. WALES'S SYMBOLS ARE _ _ _ _ _ AND _ _ _ _ _ _ _ _ _.

B. IT IS _ _ _ _'S. IRELAND'S SYMBOL IS A _ _ _ _ _ _ _ _.

C. IT IS _ _ _ _ _ _'S. SCOTLAND'S SYMBOL IS A _ _ _ _ _ _ _.

D. IT IS _ _ _ _'S. ENGLAND'S SYMBOL IS A _ _ _ _.

It's Raining!

À qui est ce parapluie ? Relie les gouttes de pluie de chaque couleur de la plus petite à la plus grande pour compléter les bulles des personnages selon leur couleur.

WHOSE UMBRELLA IS IT?

Never Mind!

Pour comprendre ce que disent Richard and Sue, écris les mots à l'endroit.

Have a Nice Trip

Sandra se prépare pour partir en vacances. Raye toutes les cases qui permettent d'écrire ce qu'elle emporte. Il te restera deux cases pour écrire ce qu'elle a oublié.

SWIM	RAIN	TO	SC
ARF	SUN	HI	PA
KING	BO	OTS	BACK
CRE	CK	GLO	AM
VES	WEL	SUIT	COAT

Solutions des jeux

Solutions

p. 5 - Nice to Meet You!

1 : D - 2 : A - 3 : B - 4 : C.

HOW OLD ARE YOU?
I AM ELEVEN YEARS OLD.

WHERE ARE YOU FROM?
I AM FROM PARIS.

WHAT IS YOUR NAME?
MY NAME IS SANDY.

WHERE DO YOU LIVE?
I LIVE IN LONDON.

p. 6 - Be Happy!

I AM A BABY.
THEY ARE HAPPY.
HE IS MY FRIEND.
IT IS A GOOD FILM.
YOU ARE LATE.
WE ARE TOGETHER.
YOU ARE MARRIED.
SHE IS SLEEPING.

p. 7 - Hello Everybody!

GOODBYE!

O - GOOD MORNING.
D - GOOD AFTERNOON.
B - GOOD EVENING.
Y - GOOD NIGHT.

p. 8 - Numbers Puzzle

p. 9 - Around the World

I AM BRITISH.
I AM IRISH.
I AM SPANISH.
I AM AUSTRALIAN.
I AM FRENCH.

p. 10-11 - Colours

THE TAXI IS BLACK.
THE SUN IS YELLOW.
THE DOG IS WHITE.
THESE BIRDS ARE PINK.
THE SKY IS BLUE.
THE PHONEBOX AND
THE LETTERBOX ARE RED.
THE GRASS IS GREEN.
THE HORSE IS BROWN.

p. 12 - So British!

EDINBURGH (SCOTLAND).
BELFAST (NORTHERN IRELAND).
DUBLIN (REPUBLIC OF IRELAND).
CARDIFF (WALES).
LONDON (ENGLAND).

BRITISH ISLES.

Solutions

p. 13 - Flags

LE DRAPEAU DU ROYAUME-UNI EST COMPOSÉ DES TROIS CROIX DE SAINT PATRICK, SAINT GEORGE ET SAINT ANDREW.

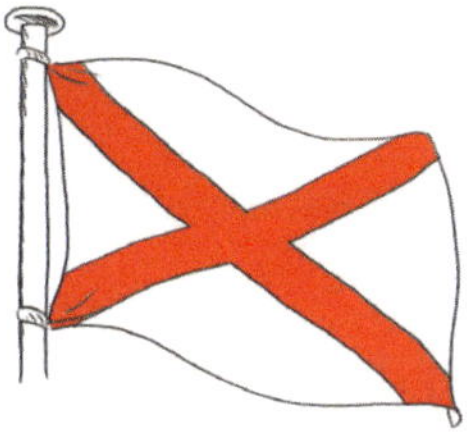

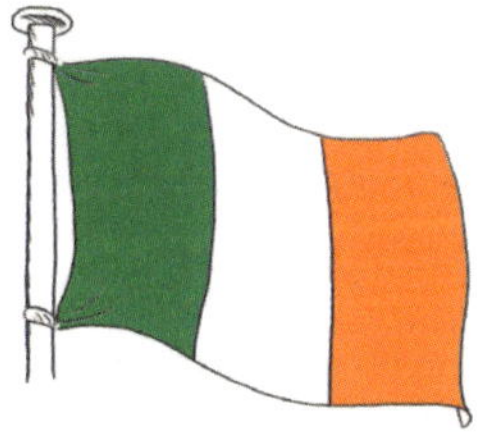

p. 14 - Happy Birthday!

MY BIRTHDAY IS ON MAY 11TH.
IT IS IN JUNE.

p. 15 - Month After Month

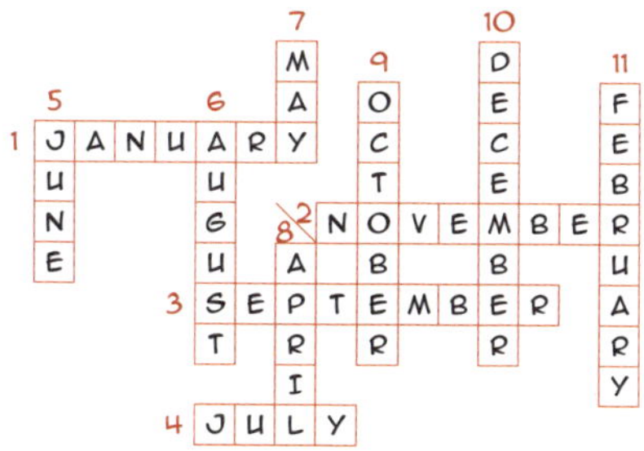

THE THIRD MONTH IS MARCH.

p. 16 - What a Mix-up!

TUESDAY,
THE TWENTY-THIRD (23RD) OF JULY.
MONDAY,
THE THIRTIETH (30TH) OF SEPTEMBER.
SUNDAY,
THE THIRTY-FIRST (31ST) OF NOVEMBER. WEDNESDAY,
THE TWENTIETH (20TH) OF MAY.

Solutions

p. 17 - Four Seasons

1 – D : IT IS SPRING, IT IS RAINING! – C'EST LE PRINTEMPS, IL PLEUT !
2 – C : IT IS WINTER, IT IS SNOWING! – C'EST L'HIVER, IL NEIGE !
3 – B : IT IS SUMMER, THE SUN IS SHINING! – C'EST L'ÉTÉ, LE SOLEIL BRILLE !
4 – A : IT IS AUTUMN, IT IS VERY WINDY! C'EST L'AUTOMNE, IL Y A BEAUCOUP DE VENT !

p. 18 - Photo Memories

EASTER IS IN SPRING.
CHRISTMAS IS ON DECEMBER, 25TH.
SAINT VALENTINE'S DAY IS ON FEBRUARY 14TH.
HALLOWEEN IS IN AUTUMN.

p. 19 - Who's Who?

IT IS NUMBER 4.

p. 20 - The Royal Family

PRINCE CHARLES
"OUR GRANDFATHER"
PRINCESS DIANA
"OUR GRANDMOTHER"
PRINCE WILLIAM
"OUR FATHER"
KATE MIDDLETON
"OUR MOTHER"
PRINCE HARRY
"OUR UNCLE"
PRINCE GEORGE
"MY BROTHER".

PRINCESS CHARLOTTE
"I AM GEORGE'S SISTER".

p. 21 - Ring! Ring!

1 – C : HOW ARE YOU FEELING? – I AM ANGRY.
2 – B : HOW IS HE FEELING? – HE IS SCARED.
3 – D : HOW IS SHE FEELING? – SHE IS HAPPY.
4 – A : HOW ARE THEY FEELING? – THEY ARE SAD.

p. 22 - The Move

WOLFY!

p. 23 - Word Mix

HE HAS GOT A BLUE T-SHIRT.
SHE HASN'T GOT A HAT.
THEY HAVE GOT A COMPUTER.

HAVE YOU GOT A CAT?
NO, I HAVEN'T.
AND HAS SHE GOT A CAT?
NO SHE HASN'T.

p. 24-25 - Party!

~~T~~	~~H~~	~~I~~	~~R~~	~~S~~	~~T~~	~~Y~~
H	~~H~~	~~U~~	~~N~~	~~G~~	~~R~~	~~Y~~
~~H~~	~~C~~	~~N~~	~~O~~	~~I~~	~~S~~	~~Y~~
~~O~~	~~A~~	A	~~S~~	~~A~~	~~D~~	P
~~T~~	~~L~~	~~T~~	~~I~~	~~R~~	~~E~~	~~D~~
P	~~M~~	Y	~~C~~	~~O~~	~~L~~	~~D~~

I AM HAPPY!

Solutions

p. 26 - So Cute!

RABBIT. GOLDFISH. PUPPY. KITTEN. GUINEA PIG.

p. 27 - Tweet! Tweet!

I HAVE GOT A FROG.
I HAVE GOT AN ELEPHANT.
SHE HAS GOT A HAMSTER.
WE HAVE GOT THE MOST BEAUTIFUL CANARY!
I HAVE GOT THE BEST CAT!

p. 28 - Jobs

1 – TRUE.
2 – FALSE : HE IS A CLOWN AND HE HAS GOT A RED NOSE.
3 – FALSE : HE IS A POSTMAN AND HE HAS GOT THE LETTERS.
4 – TRUE.

p. 29 - The Hair Salon

I AM A GIRL.
HE HAS GOT SHORT HAIR.
WE HAVE GOT BEARDS.

p. 30 - Puzzle

1 – A LITTLE BABY.
2 – A DELICIOUS CAKE.
3 – A BLACK CAT.

p. 31 - My Friends

WE ARE GOING ON FAMILY HOLIDAYS WITH OUR PARENTS.
THEY ARE RUNNING WITH THEIR NEW SHOES.
SHE IS SO PRETTY, I LOVE HER EYES.
WHAT IS YOUR NAME?
MY NAME IS LUKE.
WHO IS WITH JOHN?
IT'S HIS SISTER.

p. 32-33 - My Body and my Face

FEET.

p. 34 - My Look

A – 4 : I HAVE GOT CURLY HAIR AND FRECKLES.
B – 1 : I AM SMALL AND I HAVE GOT A BIG BLACK MOUSTACHE.
C – 2 : I AM SLIM AND I HAVE GOT LONG STRAIGHT HAIR.
D – 3 : I HAVE GOT BRACES AND MY FRIENDS DON'T THINK I AM UGLY.

p. 35 - Pretty Woman

				H	A	T				
		T	R	O	U	S	E	R	S	
					S	H	O	R	T	S
				S	K	I	R	T		
S	W	E	A	T	E	R				
			C	O	A	T				

TODAY I CHOSE MY T-SHIRT.

p. 36 - Boo!

1 – MUMMY.
2 – GHOST.
3 – WITCH.
4 – WIZARD.

p. 37 - The Match

1 – I CAN PLAY FOOTBALL.
2 – I CAN PLAY RUGBY.
3 – I CAN PLAY GOLF.
4 – I CAN PLAY TENNIS.

Solutions

p. 38-39 - Music Maestro!

BAGPIPES.

p. 40 - English Breakfast

1 - B. 2 - D. 3 - A. 4 - C.

p. 41 - Enjoy!

1 - TRUE. 2 - TRUE. 3 - FALSE. 4 - FALSE.
PLEASE, I WANT SOME CAKE.

p. 42 - Lunchbox

FISH AND CHIPS.

p. 43 - Free Time

DRAW. I HATE DRAWING.

I LIKE PLAYING VIDEO GAMES, IT'S FUN.
I LOVE PAINTING, IT'S EXCITING.
I PREFER GOING TO THE CINEMA, IT'S AMAZING.
I HATE HORROR MOVIES, THEY ARE SCARY.

p. 44-45 - Balanced Diet

I NEED MENU 2.

p. 46 - Recreation

1 - I GO TO THE ICE-RINK.
2 - I GO TO THE LIBRARY.
3 - I GO TO THE CINEMA.
4 - I GO TO THE PARK.

p. 47 - Star

HE IS THE TRAMP (CHARLOT).

I LIKE TURKEY WITH ROAST POTATOES.
AND I LOVE CHRISTMAS PUDDING, IT'S SO TASTY!

p. 48 - In the Morning

2 - NO SHE DOESN'T. SHE BRUSHES THEM IN THE BATHROOM.
3 - NO HE DOESN'T. HE GETS DRESSED IN HIS BEDROOM.
1 - NO THEY DON'T. THEY HAVE BREAKFAST IN THE DINING ROOM.

p. 49 - Ready!

I AM READY TO GO TO PLAY FOOTBALL AT EIGHT O'CLOCK.

p. 50 - Tick-tock

IT'S ONE O'CLOCK. - 01:00 A.M.
IT'S HALF PAST FOUR. - 04:30 P.M.
IT'S TWELVE O'CLOCK. - 12:00 A.M..

IL EST 3H20. IL EST 4H40. IL EST 11H25. IL EST 8H55.

p. 51 - When?

WE ALWAYS GO TO BED AT 09:00 P.M.
YOU NEVER WATCH TV IN THE MORNING.
HE OFTEN DOES HIS HOMEWORK ON SUNDAYS.
SOMETIMES WE GO TO THE CINEMA AT THE WEEKEND.

Solutions

p. 52 - Housework

C - SHE DOES NOT IRON THE CLOTHES.

p. 53 - Rules

1 - IN THIS SCHOOL, YOU MUST WEAR A TIE!
2 - YOU MUSTN'T PARK HERE.
3 - YOU MUST BE QUIET.
4 - YOU MUSTN'T DRAW ON A BOOK.

p. 54 - Yes We Can!

WATCH.
I CAN'T FIND MY WATCH.

p. 55 - It's not me...

1 S I T D O W N
2 C O M E I N
3 S T A N D U P
4 L I S T E N
5 D O N T T O U C H
6 P U T Y O U R H A N D U P
7 R E P E A T P L E A S E
8 B E Q U I E T

DON'T CHAT!

p. 56 - Geography

L	A	O	K	M	E	P	H	T
M	P	E	L	T	H	K	O	A
K	T	H	P	A	O	E	M	L
A	O	T	H	P	M	L	K	E
E	M	K	O	L	A	H	T	P
H	L	P	E	K	T	O	A	M
O	K	M	T	E	L	A	P	H
T	H	L	A	O	P	M	E	K
P	E	A	M	H	K	T	L	O

LOOK AT THE MAP.

p. 57 - Subjects

I MUST TAKE MY HISTORY BOOK.

p. 58-59 - In my Classroom

1 - A. 2 - B. 3 - A. 4 - B. 5 - B. 6 - B.
7 - A. 8 -B.

p. 60 - Timetable

ON SATURDAYS AND SUNDAYS WE DO NOT GO TO SCHOOL.
ON MONDAYS AND FRIDAYS WE MUST WEAR OUR SPORTS KIT.

Solutions

p. 61 - Hide and Seek

p. 62 - Food

1 - B. 2 - C. 3 - D. 4 - A.

p. 63 - Video Game

HOW MANY INVADERS ARE THERE?
LOOK! THERE ARE SEVENTEEN

HOW MUCH IS IT TO PLAY?

p. 64-65 - At Home

1 - IN THE GARAGE.
2 - IN THE STUDY.
3 - IN A BEDROOM.
4 - IN THE ATTIC.
5 - IN THE BATHROOM.
6 - IN THE KITCHEN.
7 - IN THE GARDEN.
8 - IN THE DINING-ROOM.
9 - IN THE LIVING-ROOM.

Solutions

p. 66-67 - In my Bedroom

							7				
	1	C	A	R	P	E	T				
				6			A			9	
			2	C	U	P	B	O	A	R	D
	5			H			L	8		A	
	L			A	3	B	E	D		D	
	A			I				E		I	
4	M	I	R	R	O	R		S		O	
	P							K			

"I NEED A COMPUTER".
TU AS DESSINÉ UN ORDINATEUR.

p. 68-69 - In Town

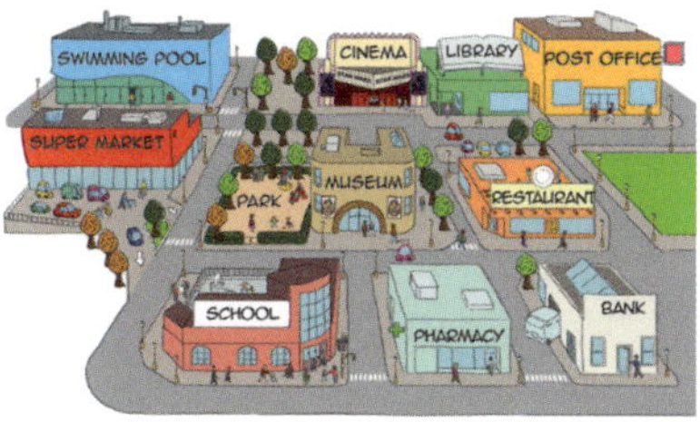

p. 70 - A Good Price

HOW MUCH ARE THEY?

p. 71 - At the Greengrocer's

CAN I HELP YOU?
LOOK, THESE BANANAS ARE EXPENSIVE
BUT THOSE PINEAPPLES ARE CHEAP.
NO THANK YOU.
I WANT THIS RED APPLE
BUT NOT THAT GREEN ONE.

p. 72 - Cheers

1 - JOHN IS OLDER THAN LESLEY.
2 - SANDRA IS PRETTIER THAN DONALD.
3 - DIDIER IS MORE AMUSING THAN LYDIA.
GLEN IS BIGGER THAN NICOLE.

p. 73 - Woof and Meow

THE DOG IS AS INTELLIGENT AS THE CAT.
THE DOG IS NOT AS FAT AS THE CAT.

p. 74 - Shopping

1 - B : I WORK IN THE SPORTS SHOP.
2 - C : I WORK IN THE CLOTHES SHOP.
3 - D : I WORK IN THE VIDEO GAME SHOP.
4 - A : I WORK IN THE SHOE SHOP.

p. 75 - Money! Money!

I AM LUCKY, I FOUND A PENNY!

p. 76 - Famous!

WE ARE CROSSING ABBEY ROAD.

BUCKINGHAM PALACE

Solutions

p. 77 - The Weather

IT'S SUNNY.

p. 78 - Wow!

YESTERDAY I WAS ON THE LONDON EYE WITH MY BROTHER AND WE WERE SCARED!

p. 79 - London

I DID NOT SEE BIG BEN.
C'EST LA PHOTO A.

p. 80 - Visit to the Zoo

DROVE.
WE CAME BACK IN A BLACK TAXI, HE DROVE TOO FAST.

p. 81 - Emblems

1 - B : IT IS RYAN'S.
IRELAND'S SYMBOL IS A SHAMROCK.
2 - C : IT IS DONALD'S.
SCOTLAND'S SYMBOL IS A THISTLE.
3 - D : IT IS JOHN'S.
ENGLAND'S SYMBOL IS A ROSE.
4 - A : THEY ARE ERWAN'S.
WALES'S SYMBOLS ARE LEEKS AND DAFFODILS.

p. 82 - It's Raining!

IT'S MINE.
IT'S YOURS.

p. 83 - Never Mind!

I AM DOING MY HOMEWORK.
CAN YOU HELP ME?
SORRY, I AM GOING TO HYDE PARK.
LOOK! IT IS RAINING...
SO, I AM GOING TO HELP YOU.

p. 84 - Have a Nice Trip

I FORGOT MY TOWEL.

Crédits photographiques :

p. 16 : Carnet : © DVARG / Shutterstock
p. 47 : Charlie Chaplin : © meunierd / Shutterstock
p. 79 : La Tamise : © Angelina Dimitrova / Shutterstock
Tower Bridge : © TTstudio / Shutterstock
Big Ben : © S.Borisov / Shutterstock
Madame Tussaud's : © chrisdorney / Shutterstock.

PAPIER À BASE DE
FIBRES CERTIFIÉES

LAROUSSE s'engage pour l'environnement en réduisant l'empreinte carbone de ses livres. Celle de cet exemplaire est de :
650 g éq. CO_2
Rendez-vous sur www.larousse-durable.fr

Dépôt légal : Avril 2016
Imprimé par Espagne Par Grafica Estella
317810/03-11035582 - avril 2017